The Beautiful Ones Have Been Born

Also by Che Chidi Chukwumerije

<u>*Poetry Collections:*</u>
Palm Lines
Writing Is The Happiness Of Sorrow
Light Of Awakening
River
Cumbrian Lines: Poems inspired by the Lake District

Mmiri a zoro nwayọ nwayọ (Igbo poems)

Der Schlaf, aus dem ich wachend träume (German poems)
Das dauerhafte Gedicht (German poems)
Innengart (German poems)

<u>*Prose:*</u>
Twice is not enough
The Lake of Love
There Is Always Something More

<u>*For children:*</u>
Somayinozo's Stories

Che Chidi Chukwumerije
The Beautiful Ones Have Been Born.
2nd Edition 2015.
1st Edition 2013 under the pseudonym Aka Teraka.
Boxwood Publishing House, e.K.
Copyright © Che Chidi Chukwumerije 2013.
All Rights Reserved.
ISBN 978-3-943000-78-8
Cover photo © Antje Renner

Che Chidi Chukwumerije

The Beautiful Ones Have Been Born

Poems on the activation
of the can-do and will-do spirit
of self-help in Africa

Boxwood Publishing House

Contents

Part 1: It Is In You   7

Build a car   9
Quantum leap   10
The beautiful ones have been born   11
It is in you   12
Sugarcane   14
When you're born, it's your turn   15
The inner road   16
You have to love your people   17
Speak your mind before you die   18
This generation   19
The future   20
Tired of doing nothing   21
I don't want to be a trader   22
Happiness   23
Trust   24

Heaven on earth   25

Part 2: On Your Marks   27

Land of spirits   29
Stillborn in the cradle of humanity   30
Life is a burden made light   31
Intimacy   32
Bitter fruits   33
Do not be afraid of unity   34
Independent Farmer   35
Light logic   36
What are you doing?   37
Movement   38
Defeat   39
Vampires   40
In light of this   41
On your marks   42
We were given wing   43
13th moon   44

1.

It Is In You

Build A Car

Running down the ladder of time
Two at a time backwards
Strangers cook the food in your stomach
How can you vomit what
You cannot digest? You cannot even
Build a car, you cannot even
Drive to the future where the world has gone
You cannot even think about it
You are waiting to buy a thinking cap
Discarded by somebody else's yesterday.

Quantum Leap

The plane that flew away
You cannot follow with your spear
The air is too far

The train that raced away
You cannot track with walking stick
The rails have melted into walking recycle

They can lend you money
With which to buy from them
What money cannot make –

It comes from the spirit
Awaken, black spirit, and take
The quantum leap

Don't read it. Think it.
Don't buy it. Make it.
Don't take it. Give it.

There is something greater than
Independence. It is called
Self-dependence. Adulthood.

The magic bridge built by children yesterday
You cannot cross on adult feet
Firm enough to take the leap today.

You have to leap forward.

The Beautiful Ones Have Been Born

A beautiful one was born
Was told
The beautiful ones have not
Been born

He sat on the ground
And waited
For the coming of those
For whom he has neglected
To prepare the way.

An ugly one was born
Was told
Yours is the land, for
The beautiful ones have not been born

He grasped the spear of destiny
Stabbed it into the land
Until the land bled blood and oil
And bowed to him who had been bold enough
To take possession of it.

The beautiful one gave birth
To another beautiful child, and said
To it mournfully: the ugly ones
Still rule over our land
And the beautiful ones have not
Been born.

It Is In You

I had a dream
I saw a man
With a sign
Around his neck

Upon the sign
Bold and bright
Was writ the words
Third world.

The more I looked
The more I saw
That he was searching
For something

And all he met
He begged for food
For water, for roof
And for directions

Helped by charity
He searched and searched
Until he saw
The thing he sought

He stood before
A yearning gulf
That separated him
From a distant land

Above the land
In glittering gold
Was writ the words
First world.

He looked around
To find the bridge
To cross the gulf
But there was none

He stretched his hand
Towards the gulf
To his surprise
He touched a mirror

I had a dream
I saw a man
Who stopped and looked
Within himself.

Sugarcane

Sugar cane is
To say
I was happy to be hungry
In a foreign land of plenty
As long as the sugar cane I planted
Back home was growing my people
And sweetening their lives.

When You're Born, It's Your Turn

When you're born
It's your turn
To feel the pain of
Rivers of gutters

When you're born
It's your turn
To be torn between
Tribe, faith and country

When you're born
It's your turn
To define the struggle
And decipher the next step

When you're born
It's your turn
To join the cause
And continue the fight

To try to solve the riddle
That baffled your ancestors
Step by step
One generation after the other

Believe, brother, believe
Courage, sister, courage
Our time is the time
We have been waiting for

Now you're born
It's your turn
Feel the weight of the work
And the lightness of hope.

The Inner Road

The seeker who
Travelled from nation to nation
Stood still
By the side of the inner road.

The seeker who
Journeyed from third world to first
Stood still
By the side of the inner road.

The seeker who
Sojourned upon the inner road
All he did was stand his ground
And build his country up.

You Have To Love Your People

You have to love your people
With a hopeful love
That sees the future
Outlive the past

You have to love your people
With a severe love
That sees their faults
In the light of truth

You have to love your people
With a gentle love
That wipes their tears
Reopening their eyes

You have to love your people
With a mysterious love
That makes them wonder
Why your love never dies.

Speak Your Mind Before You Die

The rains are coming, drumming
Thunderclouds ominously humming
Summing up your life like a gathered fist
Raised to be smashed one last time
A thunderclap, torrential downpour, tropical rain
Will wash away the soil, your time is up.

Short was your life, following other people
Fitting in, swallowing your saliva; activated one,
Do not go like this; open your mouth
And speak your mind before you die.

This Generation

This generation
Will not pass away
Without passing your way

Will you join the train
Or will you
Miss the point?

The shout of dawn
Deafens the walking dead
Only insomniacs brave the restlessly

Rising sun.

The Future

The future is
Not in the hands of
Children.
Men, stand up and do your work.

Shame upon him
Who burdens a child
With the responsibility of adults.

The future is
Not in the hands of
Children –
It is in
The hands of adults.

Tired Of Doing Nothing

Are you tired of doing
NOTHING
In a world where many things
Are happening every day?

Are you tired of making
NOTHING
In a world where many things
Are being made every day?

Good morning. Did you sleep well?

I Don't Want To Be A Trader

Dear Uncle Okeke
I don't want to be a trader
Like you.

Uncle, before you disinherit me,
An ungrateful nephew
Whose way through school
You paid
With the fruits of your trade,
Ask yourself
Who made all these things
You buy and sell.

My brother Okafor
Whose way through school
You also paid
By trade
Can go into trading like you
When he is done.

But I want to be the one
Who makes the things
He sells to others
One day.

Happiness

Happiness comes
When you fight for your people,
He said and plunged
Head first into the battle
Where he died.

A monument went up where he fell
Wet by the wistful tears of all those
Who let him fight and
Die alone.

And though they are all still alive
In comfortable compromise, yet
Happiness is gone.

Trust

Some evenings
The past rushes upon us
Like a confused wind
Looking for fruits to devour
On the branches of trees
It planted.

How can the past understand the future
When we say no the fruit
Is not yet ripe
Today is not the day to feast
We must hunger and plant some more?
Sometimes the daughters and the sons
Must say to the mothers and the fathers
You have no other choice but to trust us.

Heaven On Earth

I told a friend
Come let's go and transform
Our nation –
He told me transform yourself
And walked away
And left me burning there
With the desire in my heart.

I told a friend
Come let's ennoble our country
He told me
Seek first the kingdom of God
And walked away
And left me burning there
With the broom in my hand.

I told a friend
Come let's make our people great
He warned me
Pride goes before a fall
And walked away
And left me burning there
With my shame in my heart.

I wondered if he was not as ashamed
As I was at driving in the dark
Down badly tarred streets
In an expensive limousine
Invented, designed and built by foreigners.

If there be heaven
I want it on earth.
Come, let's transform our nation.

Che Chidi Chukwumerije

2.

On Your Marks

Land Of Spirits

Have you ever seen
Spirits spirits spirits
So many spirits in one land?

Spirit of music
Spirit of feasting
Spirit of commerce
Spirit of asking
Spirit of taking
Spirit of consuming
Spirit of boasting
Spirit of complaining

Evil spirit
Magic spirit
Fighting spirit
Family spirit
Holy Spirit
Prayer spirit
Nomadic spirit
Alcoholic spirit

Have you ever seen
Spirits spirits spirits
So many spirits in one land?

Ageing is the spirit of independence
Stillborn is the spirit of self-dependence
Missing alone is the
Spirit of discovery
Spirit of invention
Spirit of made in the land
Of the self-dependent.

Have you ever seen
Spirits spirits spirits
So many spirits missing in one land?

Stillborn In The Cradle Of Humanity

Must the first
Always be the last?
Is it a blessing or a curse?
When will the future mirror the past
We boast we had?

Must civilization end
Where it started?
How can pyramid builders after
Migration become
Moulders of huts? Is the Nile
That distant from the Niger?
No confluence point.

If we did it once, let's
Do it again. Or it would have
Been stillborn in the cradle
Of humanity.

Life Is A Burden Made Light

Life is a burden made light
By the weight of sacrifice
Your life is useless unless used to the full
For something meaningful and useful.

Self is heavy, selflessness is light
The battle is painless for them that fight
The volunteer's prize is dignity
Freedom is not for free.

Intimacy

We have wandered
But not yet that far
Away from the dawn
To have forgotten the rosy promise
Of independence morn.

The legends that awe us on paper
Were our fathers and grandfathers
In the flesh. Short is our memory
Long our vision and close to the heart
The struggle is our intimate heritage.

Bitter Fruits

It is easy to forget South Africa
When the winds of change ask us
To look ahead look ahead –
Yet the children of apartheid
Will remain growing amongst us
For a long time yet.

It is easy to forget the Congo
When the drums of globalization tempt our feet
To dance to a neutered tune –
Yet the disinherited in paradise
Will remain foraging against us
For a long time yet.

It is easy to forget Nigeria
When the rivers of democracy seduce us
Into swimming away from context –
Yet the competitors of a force-packed and divided house
Will remain wrangling amongst us
For a long time yet.

A wise farmer remembers
The seeds planted yesterday
For their bitter fruit is the food he must swallow
As he goes to work today
Planting the painful seeds of new recognition
That shall yield the hopeful seeds of tomorrow.

Do Not Be Afraid Of Unity

Brothers
Many mothers
Inherited poison
Umbilical chains
Spit out the tit
Spit out the tit!
Do not be afraid of unity.

Shadows
Treacherous arrows
The flinch
Of the clinch
Fear not illusions
Fear not delusions
Do not be afraid of unity.

The clenched fist
The strong link
The closed rank
The bound broom
The shared burden
Circle
Do not be afraid of unity.

Independent Farmer

An independent farmer
Used his ancestral land as collateral
Borrowed money from a bank
Bought agricultural equipment
Inherited secondhand from oversea

On his ancestral land
The independent farmer harvested yam
Ripe and unpeeled he sold it
To a self-dependent cook
For peanuts.

The self-dependent cook
Refined the yam into a delicious meal
Sold it back to the independent farmer
For silver and gold because
He insisted, he added value

Some have the kitchen
Some have the yam
The difference is the knowledge that
Independence is not independence
Without self-dependence.

Light Logic

I asked another friend
Come let's build our nation

She told me:
Good luck

Your reward will be in heaven
You will not see it in this Nigeria

If you want to see it
Bring light.

What Are You Doing?

Chanting monoclone beads
Roll around ominous calabash
Fermenting promises
A medicine man sits at his trade
I asked him what are you doing?
I am divining the future.

Thoughtful binoclone gaze
Intermittent glyphs startle paper and screen
Promising ferment
A restless dreamer tinkers @ his trade
I asked him what are you doing?
I am designing the future.

While some are predicting the future
Others are inventing it
What are you doing?

Movement

They will pull you back
They are afraid of...
Anything that moves!

Long shackled pain and fear
Madden the mind
Time stands still

The tempted, fallen, becomes
The tempter
Learn to recognize them

The source of your pain
The source of your freedom
Movement!

Defeat

Acceptance of ego-ineptitude
Is no humility
Even less expectation
Of it.

Even the lion who could
Not bite now hails the
Lamb his model
Yet it is his death.

Vampires

Bitten by the mosquito
Of inspiration, the venom
Of pride, youth the time-traveller
Dashes off at dawn
For dawn is the short-cut
To the future.

Something strange will happen
When it turns the corner
A crowd of stern mature faces
Worriedly authoritatively scolding
Get your head out of the clouds!
Your feet back on the ground!

Youth of today will stare
Into the face of youth of yesterday
Grown old with despair
Having learned to conform is to survive
Go with the flow
They will stop you with the power of all they've lost!

Then will you understand
The nature of the struggle that
Awaits you, my child!
If you see me too there, urging
The dream-carriers to throw off
The weight of their calling…

Remember this moment, and walk away
My child, do not stop like I did. Or
Our county will remain the same again for
Yet another generation – but
There will be one or two who whisper Believe
In your bigger dream!

In Light Of This

1st African to 2nd African:
So what do you think about Obama?

2nd African to 1st African:
The important thing is
What are you and I going to do
For Africa?

In light of this
What I suggest is:
Let us talk about our own problems
And agree on actions to tackle them
From their roots

And then let us begin
To carry out these actions
And never stop
No matter what.

3rd African irritatedly to 2nd African:
Why all this long story?
That's not the question he asked you.

2nd African:
Of course it is!
He asked me what I think about Obama
Didn't he?

On Your Marks

On a road as dusty today
As it was when his ancestor
Trailed the cock crow
Rugged hoe wedged over shoulder blade
A politician drives home
In his shiny new imported jeep
Ballot-proofed.

Only one thing has changed:
His ancestor actually heard the cock crow
And smelled the dusky moist fronds
Of dawn
And the soft earth beneath his feet
He marked with his own self-made footprints
Not with the tyre marks of imported technology.

We Were Given Wing

We were given wings
By you
Irregular wings in a new world
So we must fly

Perhaps we look ugly to you, aflight
But shall we on that account fail to fly?
Shall we, winged, remain wingless?
Shall we, pinioned, refuse the sky?

What world is it? First, second or third
It is the new world and it is ours.

13th Moon

I might be 3rd world
But I'm first nature
I might be second class
But life is my teacher

The fourth estate
Can't grow over my sixth sense
That fertile soil
Of 5-star intelligence

On the 7th day
I rest not in contentment
Even a cat 'o nine lives
Must face a tenth commandment

I will find my 8th amendment
In this eleventh hour
Will rise like the 13th moon
Of the 12 months of your year.

...

The Beautiful Ones Have Been Born

-

Poems on the activation
of the can-do and will-do spirit
of self-help in Africa

www.ingramcontent.com/pod-product-compliance
Lightning Source LLC
Chambersburg PA
CBHW030306030426
42337CB00012B/611